SANTA MONICA PUBLIC LIBRARY
I SMP 00 2237528 E
P9-CQA-142
OCEAN PARK BRANCH
Santa Monica Public Library
SEP - - 2011

Copyright © 2009 by Salvatore Rubbino

All rights reserved. No part of this book may be reproduced, transmitted, or stored in an information retrieval system in any form or by any means, graphic, electronic, or mechanical, including photocopying, taping, and recording, without prior written permission from the publisher.

First U.S. edition 2009

Library of Congress Cataloging-in-Publication Data

Rubbino, Salvatore, date.

A Walk in New York / Salvatore Rubbino. —1st U.S. ed.
p.—cm.
ISBN 978-0-7636-3855-9
1. New York (N.Y.)—Description and travel—Juvenile literature.
2. Historic buildings—New York (State)—New York—Juvenile literature.
3. New York (N.Y.)—Buildings, structures, etc.—Juvenile literature.
4. Walking—New York (State)—New York—Juvenile literature. I. Title.
F128.33.R83—2009
917.47'10444—dc22—2008020787

10 11 12 13 14 CCP 10 9 8 7 6 5

Printed in Shenzhen, Guangdong, China

This book was typeset in MKlang Bold and Futura Book.
The illustrations were done in mixed media.

Candlewick Press
99 Dover Street
Somerville, Massachusetts 02144

visit us at www.candlewick.com

A WALK IN NEW YORK

SALVATORE RUBBINO

CANDLEWICK PRESS

These trains have all arrived from the north.

Hello! This is **me**, and that's my dad! We've just arrived in Manhattan—the busiest part of New York City! Dad wants to show me around.

This platform's underground. We walk along a ramp . . .

and come up onto ground level.
"Welcome to **GRAND CENTRAL**,"
Dad says. "The largest train station
in the world!"

Wow! This hall is really huge.
And there are so many people—
all in a hurry.

Grand Central Terminal has more platforms (44) and more tracks (67) than any other railway station in the world.

The ceiling shows 2,500 stars in a night sky and the constellations of the zodiac.

The clock in the middle of Grand Central Terminal has four sides, so you can see the time wherever you are.

About 125,000 people travel to and from Grand Central Terminal every day.

New Yorkers call
the three main areas
of Manhattan
uptown,
midtown,
and downtown.

This is midtown, where
more people work than live.

We step out onto
the street, and I can't
believe my eyes!
The buildings
are so TALL;
no wonder they're
called skyscrapers.

I can tell who
the visitors are:

we're the
ones who keep
stopping to look up!

Sailors
used
to call the
sails at
the top of
ship masts
skyscrapers.

We stop again. This building's not as tall as it is WIDE.
Dad tells me it's the NEW YORK PUBLIC LIBRARY.
"And meet the library lions!" he says. "They guard the books inside."
Dad's silly—those lions aren't alive!

The New York Public Library opened in 1911 with a collection of more than one million books, including children's books.

The library lions are called Patience and Fortitude. They're made of pink marble from Tennessee.

A librarian stops to talk to us. She says 10,000 new books come in every week, and there are 88 miles of bookshelves inside!
LIC LIBRARY
The site where the library stands used to be a reservoir.
41ST
5TH AVE
TAXI

I recognize that skyscraper! It's the
Empire State Building.

"It has a hundred and two floors," Dad says. "On cloudy days you can't see the top!"

The Empire State Building isn't the tallest building in the world—but it is one of them!

Visitors can go up the Empire State Building, so Dad and I buy tickets. A policeman shows us to a high-speed elevator . . .

The Empire State Building has an observatory on the 86th floor. It's open every single day of the year.

and in less than a minute, we're 1,050 feet closer to the moon!

The Empire State Building is struck by lightning around 100 times each year, but a lightning rod at its top keeps it safe.

On a clear day you can see up to 80 miles away.

The building has 1,860 steps, 73 elevators, and 6,500 windows!

ds 1,454 feet high.

From the ground to the tip of its lightning rod, the Empire State Building sta

On foggy nights in spring and fall, the lights are turned off so that they won't confuse migrating birds.

The whole structure was built in just 410 days. It's still a record for a building of its size.

It's quiet up here, and water shines in all directions.
Dad tells me that Manhattan is an island.
He shows me some bridges that connect it
to New York's other boroughs.

New York City is made up of five "boroughs" or counties—the Bronx, Brooklyn, Manhattan, Queens, and Staten Island.

I look down, and the cars are tiny specks in the ribbon streets below.

This view faces south to New York Bay and the Atlantic Ocean.

Sal's Haulage
POLICE
51748

Back on Planet Earth, we smell a DELICIOUS smell! But to get to the hot-dog stand, we have to cross the street! Five lanes of traffic are revving at the lights. Dad puts me on his shoulders. I think he thinks that I'll be safer there.

More hot dogs are eaten in New York than anywhere else in the U.S.

macy's
Macy's is one of the oldest stores in New York. It opened in 1858.
R.H.MACY & CO.
YAP!
Yum!
Only dogs you can carry (not including hot dogs!) are allowed inside a Macy's store.
We eat our hot dogs and window-shop.
This department store is called Macy's.
Dad says that you can buy anything from a dishrag to a diamond inside.
NYC

That must be why their shopping bags come in so many shapes and sizes!

Broadway is New York's oldest and longest street. Its American Indian name is the Wickquasgeck Trail.

Now we're walking down a street called **BROADWAY**. Dad shows me an amazing skyscraper—it isn't square-shaped; it's triangular! "It's called the **Flatiron Building**," Dad says, "because it looks just like an iron."

The Flatiron Building is one of New York's oldest sky-scrapers. It has 22 floors.

Most Manhattan streets run straight, but Broadway runs diagonally.

The greenmarket in Union Square Park sells local farmers' fresh fruit and vegetables.

My feet are really tired—even Dad's are—so we find a park to rest in. It's called UNION SQUARE PARK. *We buy some fruit and postcards at a market stall, then sit down in the grass and listen to the music.*

This statue in Union Square Park of George Washington on his horse is made of bronze. It's the oldest sculpture in all the New York City parks.

After our energy comes back, we want to see some more! The streets around the park are quieter and smaller.

Dad says the buildings here are mainly homes, not offices. People know one another, and when they talk, we hear lots of different languages.

Around 170 different languages are spoken in New York.

Many old apartment buildings have iron stairways down the outside walls in case of fire and water towers on the roof.
More people live in New York than in any other city in the U.S.
Marhabah!
Salut!
TAXI

Most Manhattan streets are known by their numbers, but the streets in Greenwich Village usually have names.

The ground under Greenwich Village is too soft to build skyscrapers on.

The Village used to be a real village that was outside New York City.

The more we walk now, the more we see the sky!

Dad asks me if I'm hungry. I always am!
"Let's have a snack," he says.
"This is **Greenwich Village**,
where you find the best cafés in New York!"

We leave the café when it's almost dark.
Dad slips down a side street that brings us to the river.
"The Hudson!" he says. "And can you see the STATUE OF LIBERTY?"

From the pier, we watch the boats. The gulls watch us, and the fishermen watch the water. The sun dips behind the statue and turns her crown to gold.

About 200 different kinds of fish live in the Hudson River.

The statue's crown has seven rays because the world has seven seas and seven continents.

The statue is more than 300 feet high and was given to New York by the people of France in 1886.

The statue is green because it's made out of copper, which doesn't stay red unless you polish it.

Manhattan is a port. Oil, molasses, cocoa beans, grain, machinery, and lots of other things pass up and down the river in ships and tanker barges.

The Hudson is a tidal river, and its American Indian name is Muhheakantuck, which means "water that flows both ways."

"Taxi! TAXI!" Dad yells.
"Grand Central, please," I say.
Through the windows, the city sparkles in the night.
Dad and I agree there's just one thing better than taking a walk in New York—and that's riding a cab back!

The only way you can catch a New York cab is if you hail it.

More than 12,000 licensed cabs work in NYC, and each one's sunshine yellow!

The New York
General Post Office
is open 24 hours a day,
seven days a week.

At the lights, the driver
shows me one last thing.
"That's the James A. Farley Building," he says.
"It has the General Post Office inside."
The writing carved around the top says,

"NEITHER SNOW, NOR RAIN, NOR HEAT,
NOR GLOOM OF NIGHT STAYS THESE
COURIERS FROM THE SWIFT COMPLETION
OF THEIR APPOINTED ROUNDS."

"What does it mean?" I ask.
"It's a promise that they'll do everything they can
to get your mail to you," Dad says.

So when we reach the station,
I write one of our postcards
and drop it in the mailbox. . . .

POSTCARD
Dear friend,
I hope one day
you'll come for
a walk in
New York, too.
x x x x
USA
To you!

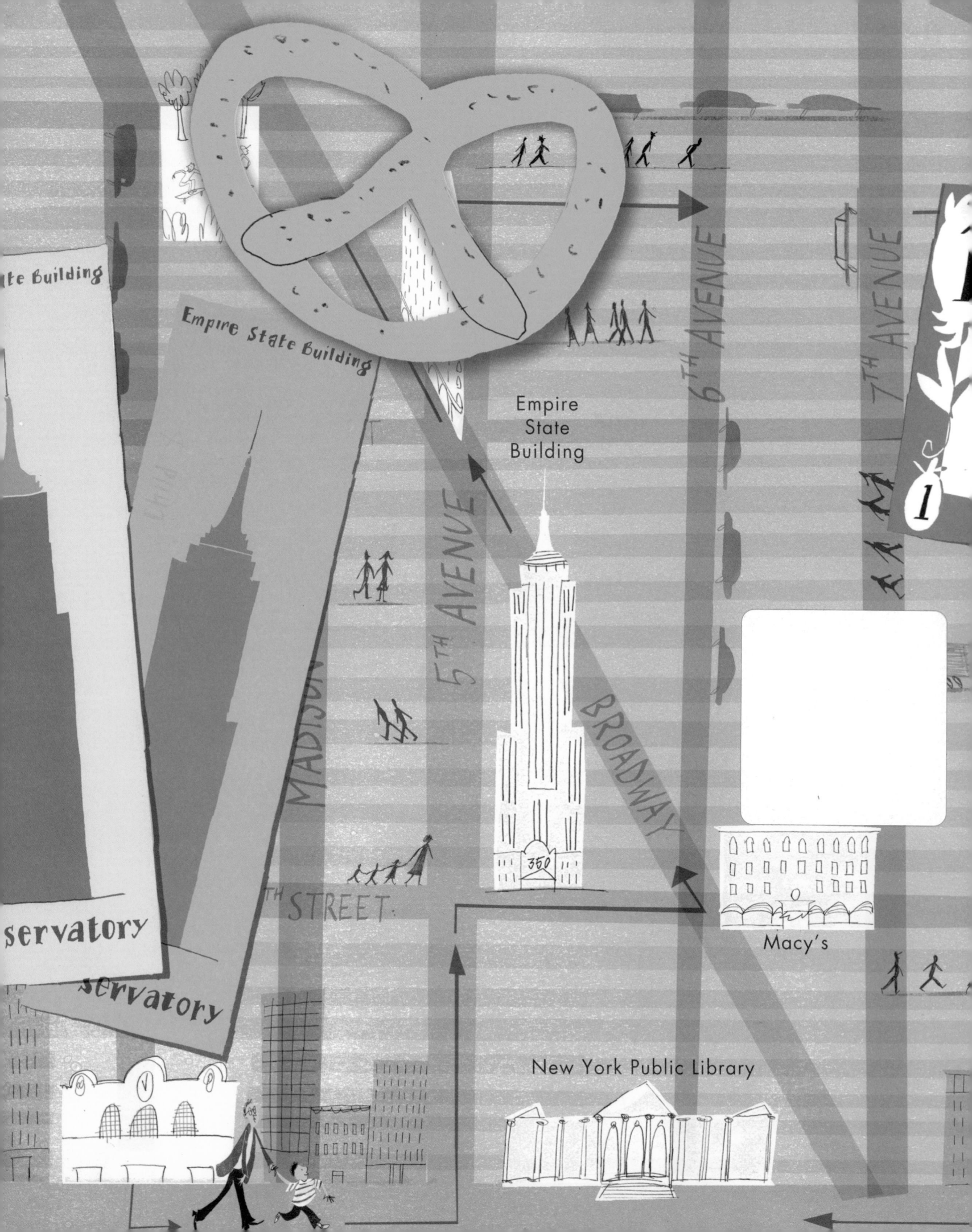
Empire State Building
Empire State Building
Empire State Building
6TH AVENUE
7TH AVENUE
5TH AVENUE
MADISON
BROADWAY
350
TH STREET
Macy's
New York Public Library
servatory
servatory